At Issue

Are Chain Stores
Ruining America?

Other Books in the At Issue Series:

At Issue

Are Chain Stores Ruining America?

Kirsten Engdahl, Book Editor

GREENHAVEN PRESS

An imprint of Thomson Gale, a part of The Thomson Corporation

Detroit • New York • San Francisco • New Haven, Conn. • Waterville, Maine • London

THOMSON

------------------*------------------ ™

GALE

Christine Nasso, *Publisher*
Elizabeth Des Chenes, *Managing Editor*

© 2006 Thomson Gale, a part of The Thomson Corporation.

Thomson and Star logo are trademarks and Gale and Greenhaven Press are registered trademarks used herein under license.

For more information, contact:
Greenhaven Press
27500 Drake Rd.
Farmington Hills, MI 48331-3535
Or you can visit our Internet site at http://www.gale.com

LIBRARY OF CONGRESS CATALOGING-IN-PUBLICATION DATA

Are chain stores ruining America? / Kirsten Engdahl, book editor.
   p. cm. -- (At issue)
Includes bibliographical references and index.
ISBN-13: 978-0-7377-3095-1 (lib. hardcover : alk. paper)
ISBN-10: 0-7377-3095-1 (lib. hardcover : alk. paper)
ISBN-13: 978-0-7377-3096-8 (pbk. : alk. paper)
ISBN-10: 0-7377-3096-X (pbk. : alk. paper)
   1. Chain stores--United States--Juvenile literature. I. Engdahl, Kirsten, 1974–
HF5468.A74 2007
381'.120973--dc22
                                                        2006019543

Printed in the United States of America
10 9 8 7 6 5 4 3 2 1

Contents

Introduction

American retail in the mid-1800s was extremely different from today's consumer landscape. Most of the stores were independent businesses owned by local townspeople. The terms "selection" and "value" were not used in connection with shopping as people had few choices about where they could make their purchases. In 1859, however, businessmen George Gilman and George Huntington Hartford established the great Atlantic & Pacific Tea Company (A&P), now considered the first American chain store. By 1931 there were more than fifteen thousand A&P stores across the United States. Throughout the twentieth century and into the present day, many more chain stores, including Woolworths, J.C. Penney's, Wal-Mart, and Barnes & Noble, have been established as major retailers in the country. There are now more than fifty thousand chains in the United States.

While many Americans have welcomed the growth of chain stores, which usually offer discounted prices and large selection, others believe that chain stores pose a threat to the American culture and economy. They argue that chain stores drive too many independent "mom and pop" stores out of business, destroy the individuality of communities, and often fail to provide fair salaries and benefits to their workers. Although the debate over the benefits and threats of chain stores may seem to be a recent one, chain stores in fact have been the subject of much controversy since they first began to proliferate in the early twentieth century.

In 1900 only fifty-eight chain stores were in business across the entire United States. By the end of the 1920s, however, the twenty leading chains had more than thirty-seven thousand stores throughout the country. A&P, the leader in the grocery segment, had more than fifteen thousand stores; J.C. Penney, an apparel chain, had approximately fourteen hundred stores; and Woolworth's had twenty-one hundred stores.

Chain stores grew because of their appeal to consumers, who appreciated the fact that they tended to be cleaner and offer more value and selection than independently run stores. Chain stores were able to offer lower prices than independents because they could purchase goods in large volumes directly from manufacturers rather than from wholesalers. After the difficult years of World War I, consumers in the Roaring Twenties were eager to enjoy themselves and the products chain stores had to offer.

As the chain stores expanded, however, so did the independent retailers' fears, who felt their very existence threatened by the booming success of chains. To combat chain stores, these smaller retailers developed "trade-at-home" campaigns in more than four hundred communities. Anti-chain store activists began urging shoppers to spend their money at locally owned stores rather than patronizing chain stores and sending money out of the community. For example, the local chamber of commerce in Springfield, Missouri, ran a trade-at-home campaign with the slogan "Keep Ozark Dollars in the Ozarks." They also ran advertisements in the newspaper *Springfield Leader* claiming that the goal of chain store managers was to "get Springfield's money and send it to the home office." Independent retailers also argued that once chain stores had taken over commerce in a community, they would raise their prices.

Leaders of the anti–chain store movement also campaigned for state and federal laws to limit the power and growth of chain stores by imposing special taxes or license fees on them. As business analyst Philip Mattera states, "Activists paved the way [for legislation] by arguing that the chains were not paying their fair share of state and local taxes. This made it easier for the movement to push for taxes (or license fees) to be imposed on chains, which were designed mainly to discourage their growth rather than simply getting them to shoulder more of the fiscal burden." Ultimately, twenty-seven out of forty-eight of the states during the interwar period enacted such tax laws, though many have since been repealed.

One of the biggest opponents of chain stores in Congress was representative Wright Patman of Texas. In 1938 he proposed legislation for a heavy tax on interstate chain stores. The tax would have exceeded the total profits for many of the stores and was intended to bankrupt these stores and put them out of business. The opposition to Patman's bill was fierce, and the proposed legislation was eventually defeated.

Chain stores tried to mobilize against the growing anti-chain store movement and legislation by forming the National Chain Store Association (NCSA) in the late 1920s. The NCSA attempted to improve the public perception of chains and lobbied against laws and taxes that threatened chain stores. The largest chain stores also made major individual efforts to combat anti-chain store laws. The A&P, for example, bought space in thirteen hundred newspapers to campaign against increased taxation of chain stores. Although some stores suffered financial loss as a result of the anti-chain store movement and punitive tax measures, many chain stores continued to thrive. As Mattera notes, "There is little evidence that the tax measures succeeded in slowing down the spread of the chains. In fact, an argument can be made that they actually strengthened the larger chains in relation to the smaller groupings, which were less able to absorb the added cost."

Since the 1930s chain stores have continued to expand and now are part of every service industry in America, including finance, insurance, and hospitality—as well as the more traditional sectors of drugstores, groceries, and apparel. As chain stores have developed, the debate over their expansion has also grown and widened. As in the 1920s and 1930s, some people today argue that chain stores benefit local communities by offering low prices and increased selection, while others believe that chain stores are harmful because they drive locally owned stores out of business. In *At Issue: Are Chain Stores Ruining America?* the authors explore these long-standing debates as well as more recent ones, including the effect of chain stores on the environment, the issue of worker exploitation, and the impact of chain stores on the character and culture of local communities.

1

Chain Stores Harm America

Mark Morford

Mark Morford is a frequent columnist for the SF Gate *and the* San Francisco Chronicle. *He is also a two-time winner of the annual National Society of Newspaper Columnists online category award.*

The overdevelopment of big-box chain stores is destroying the individuality and personality of communities across the country. The sameness of the products sold at these chain stores trains consumers to crave the comfort of conformity and fear that which is unique or different. Sadly, this homogeneity is becoming the norm and is deliberately strived for in the United States. The proliferation of soul-deadening chain stores is a plague that is eating away at the spirit of America.

Do you want to feel like you might as well be in Tucson or Boise or Modesto or Wichita or Muncie and it no longer freakin' matters, because we as a nation have lost all sense of community and place? Why, just pull over, baby. Take the next exit. Right here, this very one.

Ah, there it is, yet another massive big-box mega-strip mall, a giant beacon of glorious community decay, a wilted exclamation point of consumerism gone wild. This is America. You have arrived. You are home. Eat it and smile.

There is the Target. There is the Wal-Mart and there is the Home Depot and the Kmart, the Borders and the Staples and

Mark Morford, "One Happy Big-Box Wasteland," *SF Gate*, August 17, 2005. © 2006 SF Gate. Republished with permission of SF Gate, conveyed through Copyright Clearance Center, Inc.

the Sam's Club and the Office Depot and the Costco and the Toys 'R' Us and of course the mandatory Container Store so you may buy more enormous plastic tubs in which to dump all your new sweatshop-made crap.

What else do you need? Ah yes, food. Or something vaguely approximating it. There is the Wendy's and the Burger King and the Taco Bell/KFC hybrid (ewww) and there is the Mickey D's and the Subway and the Starbucks and the dozen other garbage-food fiends lined up down the road like toxic dominoes, all lying in wait to maul your arteries and poison your heart and make you think about hospitals.

Anyone over 30 has seen the plague evolve from a mere germ of disease in the late '80s to a full-blown pestilence of big-box shopping hell.

And here's the beautiful part: This snapshot, it's the same as it was 10 miles back, same as it will be 10 miles ahead, the exact same massive cluster of insidious development as you will find in roughly 10,000 noncommunities around the nation and each and every one making you feel about as connected to the town you're in and the body you inhabit as a fish feels on Saturn. In the dark. In a hole. Dead.

Chain Stores Have Blighted American Towns

You have seen the plague. I have seen the plague. Anyone over 30 has seen the plague evolve from a mere germ of disease in the late '80s to a full-blown pestilence of big-box shopping hell. I was recently up in northern Idaho, where my family has owned a beautiful house on a lake in a tiny burg near the Canadian border for 40 years, and to get to this region you must pass through the explosively grown resort town of Coeur d'Alene, and the plague is there perhaps worse than anywhere within a 75-mile radius.

I am officially old enough to remember when passing through Coeur d'Alene meant stopping at exactly one—*one*—traffic light on Highway 95 on the way north, surrounded by roughly one million pine trees and breathtaking mountain vistas and vast, calming open spaces, farms and fields and sawmills and funky roadside shops and gorgeous lakes for miles.

There are now about 20 traffic lights added in as many years, scattered down a 10-mile stretch of highway and each and every one demarcates a turnoff into a massive low-lying horribly designed strip mall, tacky and cheaply built and utterly heartless, and clearly zero planning went into any of these megashops, except to space them so obnoxiously that you have to get back in your goddamn car to drive the eighth of a mile to get to the Target to the Best Buy to the Wal-Mart to the Super Foods and back to your freakin' sanity.

The upsurge of soulless big-box shops . . . has, in turn, led to a deadly sense of prefabricated, vacuous sameness wherever we go.

Do you want to know what depresses the American spirit? Do you want to know why it feels like the center cannot hold and the tyranny of mediocrity has been loosed upon our world? Do you want to know what instills more thoughts of suicide and creates a desperate, low-level rage the source of which we cannot quite identify but which we know is right under our noses and which we now inhale Prozac and Xanax and Paxil by the truckload to attempt to mollify?

I have your answer. Here it is. Look. It is the appalling spread of big-box strip malls, tract homes like a cancer, meta-developments paving over the American landscape, all creating a bizarre sense of copious loss, empty excess, heartless glut, forcing us to ask, once again, the Great All-American

Question: How can we have so damned much but still feel like we have almost nothing at all?

Towns Without a Soul

Oh and by the way, Coeur d'Alene has a distinct central portion of town, well off the toxic highway. It is calm and tree lined and emptily pretty and it is packed with, well, restaurants and art galleries. And real estate offices. For yuppies. Because, of course, there are no local shops left. No mom-and-pops, few unique small businesses of any kind. No charm. No real community per se. Just well-manicured food and mediocre art no true local can actually afford and business parks where the heart used to be.

I have little real clue as to what children growing up in this sort of bizarre megaconsumerist dystopia will face as they age, what sort of warped perspective and decimated sense of place and community and home. But if you think meth addiction and teen pregnancy and wicked religious homogeny [*sic*] and a frightening addiction to blowing s--- up in violent video games isn't a direct reaction to it, you're not paying close enough attention.

This is the new America. Our crazed sense of entitlement, our nearly rabid desire for easy access to mountains of bargain-basement junk has led to the upsurge of soulless big-box shops, which has, in turn, led to a deadly sense of prefabricated, vacuous sameness wherever we go. And here's the kicker: We think it's good. We think it helps, brings jobs, tax money, affordable goods. We call it progress. We call it choice. It is the exact opposite.

A Plague of Sameness

Result No. 1: Towns no longer have personality, individuality, heart. Community drags. Environment suffers. Our once diverse and quirky and idiosyncratic landscape becomes ugly and bland and vacuous and cheap.

Result No. 2: a false sense of safety, of comfort, wrought of empty sameness. We want all our goods to be antiseptic and sanitized and brightly lit and clean. In a nation that has lost all sense of direction and all sense of pride and whose dollar is a global joke and whose economy is running on fumes and whose goods are all made overseas and whose incompetent warmongering leader makes the world gag, that toxic sameness is, paradoxically, reassuring.

Result No. 3: We are trained, once again, to fear the different, the Other, That Which Does Not Conform. We learn to dislike the unique, the foreign, foreigners. We lose any sense of personal connection to what we create and what we buy and I do not care how cheap that jute rug from Ikea was: When they are mass-produced in 100,000 chunks in a factory in Malaysia, it ain't quirky.

Sameness is in. Sameness is the new black. It is no different than preplanned Disney World vacations or organized religion or preplanned cruises or themed restaurants where all edges have been filed off and every experience has been predigested and sanitized for your protection because God forbid you have an authentic experience or nurture genuine individual perspective or dare to question the bland norm lest your poor addled soul shudder and recoil and the Powers That Be look at you as a serious threat.

I have seen the plague and so have you. Hell, you're probably shopping in it. After all, what choice do you have?

2

Chain Stores Benefit America

Pamela Villarreal

Pamela Villarreal is a research associate for the National Center for Policy Analysis. She writes articles about political, economic, and social issues.

Although critics argue that big-box chain store retailers harm local stores and exploit workers, in fact these stores provide many benefits. They increase local sales, create more jobs, and increase labor productivity nationwide. In addition, because chain stores are able to afford advanced technologies such as optical inventory scanners, they are able to operate at reduced cost and therefore offer lower prices to consumers.

Neighborhoods, city councils and the media are debating whether to welcome or discourage big-box retailers. While Wal-Mart comes to mind, big-box retailers are defined as any free-standing store greater than 50,000 square feet, and most big-box stores now range in size from 90,000 to 200,000 square feet. Critics claim that large retailers crowd out mom-and-pop competitors and replace them with windowless warehouses filled with minimum wage workers. Big-box retailers promise economic benefits such as sales tax revenues, jobs, competitive wages and low prices. But do they deliver? Empirical evidence shows that they have provided numerous benefits.

Over the past 50 years, increasing mobility has made it possible for people to shop greater distances from where they live or work. The increased competition for customers necessitated larger stores. David Boyd of Denison University argues that changing regulations also facilitated the spread of large retailers. Until the federal Consumer Goods Pricing Act of 1975, manufacturers could establish minimum prices at which their products must be sold by retailers. Such resale price maintenance severely limited price competition. The current law, however, allows mass merchandisers to provide manufacturers' products at a lower price.

West Virginia counties with Wal-Mart stores experienced a permanent net gain of about 55 retail jobs, on the average.

Big-Box Benefit: Increased Local Sales

[Researcher] Kenneth Stone of Iowa State University found that retail sales dollars from adjacent counties are lost to counties with big-box stores. In a study on the impact of Menards home improvement stores on Iowa counties, Stone concluded:

- Counties with Menards stores averaged about $21 million more in sales six years after the store opened compared to adjacent counties.

- Adjacent counties lost about $5 million in sales, on the average, indicating that consumers were crossing county lines to shop at Menards.

Stone also found the effect of Wal-Mart supercenters in Mississippi was similar. Furthermore, he discovered that some stores not in direct competition with Wal-Mart, such as high-end furniture stores, experienced greater sales due to the increase in shoppers attracted to the nearby Wal-Mart.

Big-Box Benefit: More Jobs

Critics assume that the greater competitive edge of big-box retailers comes from their ability to hire fewer workers and pay them less. However, empirical evidence has not found this to be true.

- Marshall University professor Michael Hicks found that West Virginia counties with Wal-Mart stores experienced a permanent net gain of about 55 retail jobs, on the average.

- A University of Missouri study of 1,749 counties nationwide showed that Wal-Mart counties experienced a permanent net gain of 50 retail jobs.

- Bates College researchers Brian Ketchum and James Hughes showed that Wal-Mart host counties in Maine experienced a net gain in weekly retail wages of $8.24 relative to non-Wal-Mart counties. While this is not statistically significant, it confirms that Wal-Mart did not lower retail wages.

The West Virginia study also revealed that Wal-Mart host counties experienced an average net increase of five new retail firms. Researchers refer to this as the "travel substitution effect": shoppers who previously drove to larger urban areas now have the incentive to shop in their own town, prompting new firms to cluster around big boxes.

Big-Box Benefit: Increased Productivity

Nationwide, big-box retailers have increased labor productivity, as measured by retail sales per employee:

- Between 1990 and 1999, much of the productivity growth in general merchandise stores was attributed to larger stores and greater use of "point of sale" technology, such as scanners.

- From 1995 to 1999, labor productivity grew 2.3 percent annually, compared to only 1 percent annually between 1987 and 1995.

- One quarter of the 1.3 percentage point increase in productivity came from the retail sector, and one-sixth of this was mainly due to Wal-Mart.

Since Wal-Mart began the push toward efficient distribution, other stores have copied its practices. Big-box retailers have an efficiency advantage: larger stores can house a greater selection of goods, encouraging more purchases by consumers and more sales per square foot, which enables them to reap economies of scale.

Although big-box stores create a highly competitive environment that can crowd out smaller stores, they also reduce prices.

Big-Box Benefit: Lower Prices

Although big-box stores create a highly competitive environment that can crowd out smaller stores, they also reduce prices. Analyzing 102 urban, suburban and rural areas nationwide (with and without Wal-Mart supercenters), a study from the University of Texas at Dallas recently found the presence of a supercenter was associated with a 1.36 point decline in the Consumer Price Index (CPI) for groceries, even when controlling for local differences in the cost-of-living.

Moreover, a recent study from the National Bureau of Economic Research reveals the CPI does not completely reflect price changes when big-box stores such as Wal-Mart replace other stores. In other words, if a new Wal-Mart replaces a competitor, the Bureau of Labor Statistics survey is not adjusted to reflect the lower prices of the new store. This phenomenon is known as "consumer substitution bias" in the

CPI. It results in an overstatement of the grocery inflation rate by about 15 percent annually.

The evidence that big-box retailers bring lower prices is not surprising. The cost of re-stocking goods is lower in large stores that use advanced technology, such as optical scanners, in their distribution systems. They pass these cost savings on to consumers.

Undoubtedly, as retail evolves and reduces market inefficiencies, small retailers will be affected. But evolving industries are nothing new; transportation, health care and other industries look far different than they did even a few decades ago. The efficiencies and market benefits brought by big box retailers should not be ignored in community debate.

3

Chain Stores Harm the Environment

Sierra Club

The Sierra Club is a nonprofit environmental organization founded in 1892. Its members work to ensure healthy communities and a healthy planet. The club promotes education on clean energy, the protection of nature, and the dangers of industrial pollution and encourages people to speak out against threats to their communities.

Big-box or chain stores threaten the environment. These rapidly proliferating stores take up large parcels of land with massive, paved parking lots. These impermeable parking surfaces produce a great deal of polluted runoff during rainstorms. Furthermore, when Wal-Mart and other supercenters build on the fringes of a town, traffic and toxic exhaust increase. Chain stores also force small neighborhood stores out of business, forcing consumers to drive long distances to shop and increasing the demand for more roads and development. Supporting local businesses and speaking out against environmental lawbreakers can minimize the impact of chain stores.

"Big box" stores like Wal-Mart threaten our landscape, our communities and the environment by building on the fringe of town, paving vast areas for stores and parking lots, and undermining the economic health of existing downtown shopping areas. These mega-stores are proliferating at an alarming rate, with the world's largest corporation, Wal-Mart, being the leading example of big box developments that con-

Sierra Club, "How Big Box Stores Like Wal-Mart Effect the Environment and Communities." Reproduced by permission of Sierra Club Books.

tribute to sprawl in our communities. With annual profits of over $10 billion, an amount exceeding the gross domestic product of 95 countries, Wal-Mart is on an aggressive drive to open new stores. In 2006, Wal-Mart expects to add more than 300 new stores to the existing more than 3000 discount stores, super-centers and Sam's Clubs in the United States alone.

Across the country, Sierra Club chapters and groups have opposed construction of Wal-Mart stores for a range of reasons including wetlands destruction, flooding potential and concerns about increased traffic and impacts on locally owned stores. Today, a broad range of organizations, from churches and labor unions to small businesses and environmental groups, are coming together to highlight Wal-Mart's effect on communities and promote positive solutions.

The sheer size of these giant stores and parking areas cause problems from increased traffic congestion to water pollution.

Water Pollution

The sheer size of these giant stores and parking areas cause problems from increased traffic congestion to water pollution. Wal-Mart super-center stores span several acres, and the parking lots can be three times the size of the stores, bringing the total footprint to more than 18 acres. Large parking lots contribute directly to non-point source water pollution [polluted runoff], which is the leading cause of water pollution in the U.S. Each acre of impermeable parking surface produces runoff of 25,000 gallons of water during a 1 inch storm. By contrast, a one-acre undeveloped site only has runoff of 2,700 gallons during the same storm. Runoff from impermeable surfaces leads to erosion, flooding, and the flow of pollutants like oil, chemicals, bacteria and heavy metals into waterways.

In addition, Wal-Mart has been the target of various government actions to enforce the Clean Water Act [which sets pollution standards for industry]. Since 2001, Wal-Mart has paid settlement costs and civil penalties totaling more than $8 million resulting from federal Environmental Protection Agency storm water cases. This includes Wal-Mart's payment of $3.1 million in 2004 to settle Clean Water Act cases in 9 states.

In August 2005 in Connecticut, Wal-Mart agreed to pay $1.15 million for threatening rivers and streams with chemical pollution. This included $600,000 in civil penalties for alleged violations of clean-water laws at 22 stores. Connecticut's Attorney General, Richard Blumenthal, noted at the time: "Wal-Mart's environmental record here seems as low as its prices," and announced that the company had "systematic, repeated violations across the state."

Traffic, Sprawl and Blighted Landscapes

In 2005, Wal-Mart reported having over 3,000 U.S. stores, including 242 new super-centers and a total of 459.2 million square feet of selling space. By 2015, Wal-Mart expects to occupy more than 215 square miles, an area more than 4 times the size of the city of Boston. In addition to the number of stores that exist today, Wal-Mart has blighted our national landscape with hundreds of empty store shells and thousands of acres of unused parking lots across the country.

For every super-center that opens, two neighborhood supermarkets close.

Wal-Mart and other big box retailers typically develop stores at the fringes of towns, which are accessible mainly by driving and often result in increased traffic. The huge service area for a super-center draws customers from long distances, and places significant stress on regional road and freeway systems. More traffic on the road contributes to air pollution, water contamination, and the demand for more roads and development.

The big box model can also force out other stores, threatening the economic vitality of existing downtowns and neighborhood shopping areas. Ten years after Wal-Mart came to Iowa, Professor Ken Stone of Iowa State University estimated 7,326 local businesses closed in the state's small towns and rural areas due to big box retailers. Not only does this phenomenon make for less of a traditional, walkable community with local flavor, it contributes to a pattern of development that fuels sprawl and forces more people to drive longer distances.

Retail Forward, a market research firm in Columbus, Ohio, has examined the impact of super-centers and found that for every super-center that opens, two neighborhood supermarkets close. Since many neighborhood shopping centers are anchored by supermarkets, if the supermarket closes, neighboring businesses that rely on foot traffic are also threatened. Communities can be left with vacant shopping centers, creating blight and driving down property values.

Solutions

The Sierra Club believes that because these retailers leave a large footprint on the environment, Wal-Mart and other big box stores should comply with all environmental laws and meet environmental and community standards including:

- Respect the wishes of local communities
- Do not seek or accept public subsidies or zoning waivers
- Fully disclose the environmental impact of stores and products
- Fully disclose all environmental and labor conditions of factories or sub-contractors

- Do not locate stores in wetlands, floodplains or other sensitive areas or in places that would exacerbate traffic, increase air pollution, or contribute to scattered sprawl development

- Provide infrastructure for bicycles, pedestrians and transit-users at all stores

- Reduce energy consumption through green building standards

- Restore or remove empty, abandoned stores within one year of closure

- Reduce storm water pollution by designing parking that does not rely on large lots with impermeable surfaces

We all support livable neighborhoods, good jobs and reasonable shopping choices. Big box stores with huge parking lots like Wal-Mart threaten our communities, our jobs, and our quality of life. There is a better way—demand more from big box retailers, join with community groups to challenge environmentally harmful development, and support local businesses that invest in downtowns.

4

Chain Stores May Help the Environment

Daniel Akst

Daniel Akst has written articles for many publications, including the Los Angeles Times, the Wall Street Journal, the Boston Globe, the Christian Science Monitor, and the Washington Monthly. He now writes a monthly column for the New York Times.

Most environmentalists believe that chain stores harm the environment by promoting resource consumption and covering the landscape with ugly buildings. Chain stores, however, can actually be good for the environment. For example, large chain stores offer one-stop shopping that reduces the need for many car trips, and bulk buying at warehouse stores means less packaging. Also, chain stores help make the developing countries of the world richer by buying from and producing goods in these countries. In the long run, countries with more money are better able to protect the environment.

To some environmentalists, the shoppers of the world have nothing to lose but their chains. If only people stopped spending at these awful big-box stores, the thinking goes, the earth might be saved—and local businesses would flourish.

From an environmental perspective, there is in fact much to dislike about the chains. Their low prices, sustained by a rapidly globalizing economy, promote resource-churning consumerism. They are typically reached only by auto, and thus inspire millions of greenhouse-gas-spewing car trips. And surrounded by a sea of parking lots, they are anchors of the sprawling new suburbs many of us love to hate.

But the case against the chains is not nearly so clear-cut—if you'll pardon the expression—in these tree-hugging precincts. My own view is that, from a save-the-earth standpoint at least, shopping at these stores isn't evil. It may even make the environment better.

Bear in mind, first of all, that chain stores didn't only just appear. Sears and Montgomery Ward, to name two, cropped up in the late 19th century. They were innovative and dominating retailers in their heyday, and while today we find the former quaintly harmless (the latter is dead and buried), it's worth remembering that once upon a time they generated some of the same antagonism that Wal-Mart does—for driving out local merchants, for example. In the 1920s, these mail-order businesses began sprouting brick-and-mortar branches on Main Streets all over America—in the days when people walked and rode transit. Eventually they did follow their customers to suburbia, but their early history shows that it's possible to be a chain in a world with a set of transportation options and land-use policies quite different from today's.

By offering only giant quantities, Sam's Club minimizes both shopping trips and packaging—it doesn't even offer grocery bags.

Yes, today's stores are bigger. But the point is, multi-outlet retailers simply aren't to blame for the car-oriented society in which we find ourselves; and different zoning (to say nothing of different consumer preferences) could produce a very different retailing environment, chain ownership notwithstanding.

Big Chain Stores Cut Down on Car Trips

Chain retailing, moreover, has environmental advantages. Stores like Wal-Mart and Target offer one-stop shopping for families, surely obviating many car trips. By offering only giant quantities, Sam's Club minimizes both shopping trips and packaging—it doesn't even offer grocery bags. If you hate Wal-Mart Stores Inc., Sam's parent, there is always Costco, which offers many of the same advantages plus higher wages for workers.

Large chains are also easier to monitor—and pressure— than a thousand local lumberyards or toy stores, in part because they are public companies, with all the disclosure and press scrutiny that that entails. Criticism of Wal-Mart clearly has played a role in its much-ballyhooed recent initiatives to improve environmental performance and give more employees health insurance, both arenas where small companies frankly have little to brag about. Note also how central management can rapidly change practices at thousands of stores: Home Depot now is America's biggest seller of lumber certified by the Forest Stewardship Council, and the company's size permits elaborate efforts to determine where its wood comes from and how it was harvested. The chain contends that it now knows the provenance of every broomstick and two-by-four on its shelves.

The worst thing for the global environment . . . is massive poverty.

Chain Stores Help the Ecology of Developing Nations

Another environmental knock on the chains is that they supposedly export pollution by selling so much stuff made in places with lax environmental standards (to say nothing of lax labor laws). At the very least, an awful lot of energy is expended moving products around the world to feed the global manufacturing beast. Surely it would be better to buy local.

In fact, for environmental and other reasons, it is much better not to. The main reason is that, ecologically speaking, money really matters. The worst thing for the global environment, aside from so many Americans tooling around in Ford Explorers, is massive poverty. By bringing economies of scale to the distribution of goods and leveraging the differing productive capacities of nations, modern mass merchandisers have found a good way to make the world richer—something mass merchandisers have been doing in America for more than 100 years. The resources expended transporting goods simply pale against the affluence that results. And having money is what enables us to afford a cleaner, healthier environment.

Despite our misgivings, moreover, the chains spread around this wealth. We may not envy workers in developing countries who take factory jobs, but apparently they vastly prefer these to the rural life they are leaving behind in droves. In the short term, the industrialization of those countries may lead to some environmental problems, but in the longer run it's all to the good. Economists have shown again and again that environmental conditions worsen as a country develops, only to improve again as it grows affluent enough to demand and afford cleaner water and air. It's possible that someday a country will leap past the dirty stage of development straight to a post-industrial economy, but meanwhile the model we have is better than any known alternative, on both humanitarian and environmental grounds.

"Fears that globalization necessarily hurts the environment are not well-founded," writes economist Jeffrey A. Frankel of Harvard's Kennedy School of Government. "A survey reveals little statistical evidence, on average across countries, that openness to international trade undermines national attempts at environmental regulation through a 'race to the bottom' effect."

Chain Stores Are Here to Stay

There are other social and economic arguments about the virtues and vices of chain stores, of course, all of them beyond the scope of this column. But at base, I think, a large factor in our objections to these stores—particularly in the environmental argument against them—is aesthetic. And there's no denying that looks matter; our love of nature's beauty is a big reason we care about the environment, after all. Squatting dumbly behind their vast aprons of blacktop, America's suburban chain stores are as ugly as they are banal, together comprising a built environment that exemplifies Joni Mitchell's song about paving paradise for a parking lot. And she didn't even have a verse about runoff.

Perhaps their worst offense, in other words, is that the chains represent such a drastic homogenization and dehumanization of the landscape. Sadly enough, this is the dimension of the chain-store phenomenon that is least likely to change. The simple reason is that the automobile is here to stay, even if the infernal—er, that is, internal—combustion engine is not.

Since the chains aren't about to vanish, maybe a better strategy is to go ahead and shop there. Estimate your savings each time you go, and then put that money aside. At the end of the year, you should be able to make a pretty nifty donation to the environmental cause of your choice.

5

Chain Stores Drive Out Local Businesses

Stacy Mitchell

Stacy Mitchell is an activist for locally owned businesses and does research for the New Rules Project, an organization that seeks to strengthen communities for current and future generations. Mitchell is also the author of the book Hometown Advantage: How to Defend Your Main Street Against Chain Stores and Why It Matters.

In the past decade, chain stores such as Barnes & Noble, Borders Books, Home Depot, and Lowe's have closed down thousands of local and independent stores. These local stores are unable to compete with the power of the big chains. Although some people argue that large retail corporations benefit local communities by creating new jobs, in fact they destroy as many jobs as they create. Worse, usually the lost jobs are higher-paying jobs with better benefits. Also, unlike local businesses, chain stores do not support local businesses such as banks, law offices, and computer firms. Instead, the big stores tend to deal exclusively with large national companies.

In her book, *The Death and Life of Great American Cities,* Jane Jacobs writes that what creates a sense of community is not any one particular thing, but rather the many small interactions that occur in our everyday lives.

"It grows," she writes, "out of people stopping by the bar for a beer, getting advice from the grocer and giving advice to

Stacy Mitchell, "The Hometown Advantage," speech in Saint Croix Falls, WI, October 8, 2003. © 2003 Institute for Local Self-Reliance. Reprinted by permission of the author and the author's agents, Scovil Chichak Galen Literary Agency, Inc.

the newsstand man, comparing opinions with other customers at the bakery and nodding hello to the two boys drinking pop on the stoop . . . hearing about a job from the hardware man and borrowing a dollar from the druggist . . ."

"Most of it is ostensibly utterly trivial," she goes on, "but the sum is not trivial at all. The sum of such casual, public contact at the local level . . . most of it fortuitous, most of it associated with errands . . . is a feeling for the public identity of people, a web of public respect and trust, and a resource in time of personal or neighborhood need. The absence of this trust is a disaster. . . ."

What Jacobs describes is a close-knit community built around a cohesive and vibrant local retail economy. It is a place of small stores and sidewalks. A place where commerce and community life intermix. A place where we buy goods and services from businesses owned by our neighbors.

Such places are increasingly rare. Countless cities and towns across America are now ringed by identical big box stores and acres of asphalt. Their downtowns are shuttered and vacant. Their locally owned businesses have long since disappeared, displaced by global chains that have limited ties and no long-term commitment to the community.

Since 1990, 11,000 independent pharmacies have closed.

Chain Stores Have Taken Over

The trends of the last decade are staggering. Since 1990, 11,000 independent pharmacies have closed; chain drugstores now account for more than half of all pharmacy sales. More than 40 percent of independent bookstores have failed. Barnes & Noble and Borders Books capture half of all bookstore sales. Local hardware stores are likewise disappearing. Home Depot and Lowe's control nearly 45 percent of that market. Five firms account for nearly half of all grocery sales. Blockbuster

Video rents one out of every three videos. More than 40 percent of restaurant spending is captured in the top 100 chains. Most striking of all, a single firm, Wal-Mart, now captures 9 percent of all U.S. retail sales. Wal-Mart now ranks as the largest grocer in the country, the largest toy seller, the largest furniture dealer, the largest music retailer, and the list goes on.

According to the conventional wisdom, these trends are both desirable and inevitable. We tend to assume that large retail corporations strengthen the local economy by generating new jobs and tax revenue. We assume that they benefit competition and consumers. And, even though at times we may mourn the loss of the neighborhood pharmacy or the local bookstore, ultimately we believe that there's not much we can do about it. This is simply the free market at work.

But the actual experience of many towns and cities over the last few years is at odds with the conventional wisdom. Chain retailers rarely deliver all of the benefits they claim. And these stores often entail significant hidden costs—economic as well as environmental and social.

Study after study has found that big box stores destroy about as many jobs and as much tax revenue as they create.

Retail Growth Is a "Zero-Sum-Game"

One of the things we tend to assume about big box retailers, for example, is that they create new jobs and tax revenue. And in fact they do. A 100,000 square foot store—that's about the size of a typical Home Depot—might employ 200 people and generate significant property and sales tax revenue.

But what is often overlooked is the other side of the balance sheet. Study after study has found that big box stores destroy about as many jobs and as much tax revenue as they create. This is because retail spending in a given market is a relatively fixed pie. Just because Wal-Mart builds a new outlet, it doesn't mean people are going to need more gallons of milk or pairs of socks. Unless your town is experiencing astronomical population or income growth, it's impossible to absorb one of these giant stores without causing sales to decline sharply at existing businesses, some of which will be forced to downsize or close altogether.

Dr. Kenneth Stone, an economics professor at Iowa State University, has tracked the impact of Wal-Mart and Home Depot on Iowa towns for more than a decade. His studies have consistently found that retail growth is a "zero-sum-game." That is, gains in sales at new Wal-Mart and Home Depot stores are mirrored by sales losses at existing businesses. Since Wal-Mart first entered Iowa, more than 7,000 small businesses have closed. As these businesses have disappeared, Iowa communities have lost at least as many retail jobs as the big superstores have created.

These lost jobs typically paid more with better benefits than the new jobs at the supercenter. Workers at Wal-Mart and Target supercenters earn about one-third less than employees of most supermarkets, which are unionized. Taxpayers often have to make up the difference, because many Target and Wal-Mart employees rely on food stamps and other forms of public assistance to get by.

Added Costs Outweigh New Tax Revenue

Just as the promise of new jobs often proves to be an illusion, so too does the promise of new tax revenue. When a new supercenter opens on the outskirts of town, commercial activity in the downtown declines. Over time, so too do downtown property values and tax revenue. Meanwhile, the sprawling new superstore requires substantial outlays for road maintenance, police, and other public services. It's not uncommon for these new costs, combined with the drop in downtown revenue, to actually exceed the tax revenue generated by the superstore.

Take the case in Pineville, North Carolina. This town of 3,400 people has added some 6 million square feet of retail development over the last decade. Many small towns aspire to have such a large commercial tax base in order to keep residential tax rates low. But Pineville has discovered that these stores are very costly from a public services standpoint. So much so that [in 2002] the town had to raise its residential property tax rates and suspend new retail construction in order to balance its budget.

More evidence comes from the city of Barnstable, Massachusetts, which recently commissioned a study to examine the tax impacts of different land uses. The study found that the city's big box stores and fast food outlets were costing more in services, particularly road maintenance, than they were generating in revenue. The study calculated that a 100,000 square foot big box store produced a net annual tax deficit of nearly $47,000. The study also found that the city's small Main Street businesses contribute much more tax revenue than they require in services, generating additional funds for schools, parks, and other city functions.

Local stores contribute about three times as much to the local economy as chain stores.

Local Dollars Go Further

Direct job and tax impacts are only part of what's at stake. Consider what happens to a dollar spent at a local store. Not only do profits stay in the community, but local merchants support a variety of other local businesses. They hire local accountants, printers, attorneys, web designers. They do business with the local bank. They advertise through local media outlets. They purchase goods from local producers and distributors. In this way, a dollar spent at a locally owned business creates a ripple of economic benefits and indirectly helps to support a broad range of local jobs and opportunities.

In contrast, much of a dollar spent at a chain store leaves the community immediately. Chain stores centralize all of these functions at their head offices. They keep local spending to a minimum. They bank with big national banks. They bypass local media in favor of national advertising. They deal almost exclusively with large out-of-state companies and offer few opportunities for local firms.

We recently conducted a small study of this in Maine and estimated that only 14 percent of the dollars taken in at a big box store were re-spent in the local economy. The rest left the state, flowing to corporate headquarters and out-of-state suppliers. In contrast we found that locally owned businesses returned 45 percent of their revenue to the local economy. This means local stores contribute about three times as much to the local economy as chain stores, and thus support many more local jobs and businesses.

When we think about economic development, we tend to assume that a bookstore is a bookstore, and a grocery store is a grocery store. But in fact, ownership matters. Helping a local entrepreneur get started will mean much more for the local economy than recruiting a chain.

Yet another important economic benefit of local businesses is that, in an increasingly homogenized world—where most cities and towns are overrun with the same chain stores, the same parking lots, the same kind of sprawl—those communities that have said no to cookie-cutter development and instead preserved their distinctive character and one-of-a-kind stores have an economic edge. These communities have a strong sense of local identity. They are more interesting places to live and to visit. And they are, according to a growing body of research, better able to attract entrepreneurs, relocating firms, and skilled workers, and thus are more likely to prosper over the long-term.

Chain Stores Lead to Environmental Problems

The proliferation of chain stores is not only undermining our local economies, but is also harming the environment. As the big boxes expand, more and more open space is being consumed for shopping. The amount of retail store space per capita in the U.S. has grown by more than one-third over the last 15 years. Most of this new construction has been in the form of big box stores and other large shopping centers that are accessible only by car. As a result, more and more of our daily errands now require driving, which means increased air emissions and polluted runoff into our rivers and lakes.

Locally owned businesses build strong communities.

Unlike centuries-old downtown buildings, these new shopping centers and big box stores typically last only a few years before being deemed obsolete. About one-third of all enclosed malls are now in serious financial distress. Even big box stores are going dark as companies like Target and Wal-Mart abandon existing outlets to build ever bigger stores further out. Wal-Mart alone has more than 350 vacant stores nationwide.... It is very difficult to find new uses for theses stores and they often remain vacant for years. Altogether, in the U.S., some 500 million square feet of retail space sits idle—a tremendously inefficient use of land and resources.

Local Business Is Better for the Community

One final point, and perhaps most important of all, locally owned businesses build strong communities. There's much to be said for the civic value of doing business with our neighbors—people who greet us by name, send their kids to school with ours, and have a vested interest in the long-term health of the community. Local merchants are often deeply involved in community organizations and local causes. Although we hear a lot about the charitable giving of big corporations, one study found that small businesses actually give more than twice as much per employee to charitable causes as do large companies.

Altogether, it's a pretty high price to pay to save a few bucks and even that claim may not hold up to scrutiny and time. As Barnes & Noble and Borders Books have gained market share, both chains have sharply reduced the number of books they sell at a discount. Blockbuster's rental fees are higher in markets where it has a near monopoly.

[In October 2002] the Maine Department of Human Services surveyed prescription drug prices at more than 100 pharmacies around the state. The ten lowest priced pharmacies were all independent, locally owned drugstores. National chains, including Rite Aid and CVS, had among the highest overall prices. Even more telling, prices at Wal-Mart pharmacies, which ranked somewhere in the middle overall, varied widely from one outlet to the next. Prices were lower in those markets where Wal-Mart still faces a fair amount of competition and significantly higher in those areas where it has largely eliminated local competitors.

As I've tried to demonstrate . . . much of the conventional wisdom about the benefits of chain stores is false. So too is the notion that the growth of these stores is inevitable. Although local businesses have declined in recent years, they still control a substantial share of retail spending and command a degree of love and loyalty unmatched by their corporate counterparts. More importantly, across the country, a growing number of communities are recognizing the value of maintaining local businesses and a vibrant downtown. In the last few years, hundreds of cities and towns have said no to big box retail. Many have adopted innovative land use and economic development policies to prevent chain store sprawl, strengthen locally owned retail, and revitalize their downtowns.

6

Chain Stores Benefit Local Businesses

Daren Fonda

Daren Fonda is a freelance writer living in New York. He regularly writes articles for Time *magazine.*

When chain stores come to town, it seems inevitable that smaller, local stores will soon be driven out of business. In many cases, however, chain stores actually help local stores and consumers. For example, the national advertising of businesses such as Petco creates a demand for products that benefits independent pet stores. Similarly, gourmet coffee chains such as Starbucks have shown local businesses that customers are willing to pay $4 or more for fancy coffee. As a result, independent coffee shops have been able to raise their prices and make greater profits.

Conventional wisdom would tell you Beverly's Pet Center in Pembroke Pines, Fla., should have a GOING OUT OF BUSINESS sign in its window. A family-owned shop that has sold animals and supplies since 1974, it's surrounded by hulking outlets of PetsMart, Pet Supermarket and Pet Supplies Plus. Facing the cut-rate prices of these giant chains, Beverly's was expected to get gobbled up faster than a mouse in a snake pit. But as in the wild kingdom, life in the retail jungle is full of surprises.

Beverly's turned out to be about as digestible as a porcupine. Kids love it and pester their parents to take them there. Sure, the dog food costs a little more, but they get to play with plenty of puppies, stare at exotic reptiles and marmosets, eat free popcorn, cheer hamster races and get good and scared by the predators in Beverly's 4,000-gal. shark pond. "We run a clean shop and train our employees to know what they're talking about," says co-owner Greg Rosenberg. One of Beverly's big rivals, PetsMart, abandoned a location across the street from the shop and relocated several miles away. Beverly's moved into PetsMart's old superstore [in 2001], doubling its square footage, and reports that its sales are rising 10% annually. Says Kim Paoletti, who shops there a few times a week with her two young daughters: "It's more expensive than at the chains, but the pet-food quality is better."

Independent Stores Stage a Comeback

Beverly's success is part of a feisty comeback by independent shopkeepers, and not just in the pet business. Mom-and-pop retailers in several industries—books, coffee and hardware—are prospering, sometimes literally in the shadow of popular national chains like Barnes & Noble, Starbucks, and Home Depot. This wasn't the case for much of the 1990s, when lower prices and broader selection enabled the giants to crush local shops. And to be sure, in the mass-merchandising field, Wal-Mart continues to stomp most rivals, whatever their size. But big specialty retailers today are focused more on fighting one another—and fending off Wal-Mart—than on targeting stores such as Beverly's, whose $3 million in annual sales is mere kibble to them.

These trends have left a smaller number of strong indies [independent stores] to fight for some juicy scraps. Independent bookshops have battled successfully to hold a steady 15% share of the market since 1999, says the American Booksellers Association. And despite the Starbucks blitz, the number of independent java joints has increased from 8,200 in 1999 to about 8,800 today, according to the market research firm Mintel.

Why the comeback? In part, it's survival of the fittest. Aggressive competition from the chains killed thousands of shaky retailers. Some were financially strapped and couldn't afford higher rents. Others tried to match the discounters' prices and perished. In hardware, many old-timers were not willing to invest in merchandising or such new technologies as inventory-management systems and instead let their businesses decline until they retired.

Finding Ways to Compete

The survivors in each field, however, discovered ways to compete. Almost all provide superior service. Their sales staffs know their products and customers well and stock what the locals want. They emphasize convenience and make things easy to find. Some choose specialties in which they can excel, whether it's children's books or saltwater fish. And many now employ more sophisticated pricing strategies.

Pat Sullivan, 42, owner of Sullivan Hardware shops in the Indianapolis area, is surrounded by Lowe's outlets and a Home Depot. But he steadily increases revenues 6% to 8% a year, and he books pretax margins of about 10% on $5 million in annual sales. "I'm a speck to the chains," he says, "but I do well." Over the years, he adapted his merchandise mix and pricing to cope with the big-box stores. He knows he'll never beat Home Depot and Lowe's on prices for $100-plus power tools, so he stocks a minimal quantity. Instead, he targets weekend tinkerers who need repair and maintenance goods in a hurry, and he has bulked up on lawn and garden supplies and high-end paints, which are hot growth lines on which he can earn good profits.

He also practices guerrilla pricing. Sullivan comparison-shops at the chains and tracks the smaller-ticket items they advertise, like sealant or tape measures. He prices the same merchandise about 10% to 15% higher and, like them, earns a higher margin on items that aren't so price sensitive, such as basic tool kits and paint accessories. The strategy lures customers to his store (as it does to the chains), but Sullivan wins additional business through service. His sales force helps people find the right socket wrench fast, holds their hands through a plumbing project and pays a home visit if necessary. Says longtime customer Dan Laycock: "If I need a couple of nuts and bolts, I don't want to wait behind people buying drywall." Sullivan is doing so well that he opened his fourth store just six months ago.

Sullivan owes part of his success to the advice he gets from the co-op to which he belongs, Do It Best, which has 4,128 members nationwide and provides consolidated buying power. (Other co-ops, such as Ace Hardware and TruServ, offer the same service to their members.) And the co-ops have become more savvy in advising members on ways to beat the chains.

Banding Together

In the book business, the indies are also banding together. Their American Booksellers Association established national gift certificates so that customers or their friends and family could redeem them at any member shop (of which there are 1,200, about half the nation's indies). The independents have an e-commerce site called BookSense.com to go up against Amazon.com. They display best-seller lists compiled from indie shops nationwide and benefit from a $600,000 ad budget, used for promotions in such publications as the *New Yorker* and the *Atlantic Monthly*.

Collette Morgan, owner of the children's bookstore Wild Rumpus Books in Minneapolis, Minn., says the website helped increase her sales 10% [in the] last year. But she generates plenty of her own buzz. When she opened a decade ago, she was fresh from a general-interest indie that died after a Barnes & Noble moved in across the street. Morgan decided to make her store "something a corporate mind would never dream up and that a large company could never sustain."

Her idea was to open a store that would sell children a good time along with their reading material. Wild Rumpus is part zoo, with a couple of chickens named Dalai and Elvis (which kids chase around), along with cats, tarantulas, fish and birds. Boys play poker in the store's Haunted Shack, which sits atop a Plexiglas surface that exposes a gray rat colony below. Saturday afternoons feature offbeat activities like sheep shearing. Customer Carrie Watson's toddler Isabel loves the Monday story readings and the animals. "I would much rather visit an independent than a large store anyway," says Watson.

Morgan charges the cover price for her books, while the big boxes often discount, but she carries hundreds of titles they don't stock. Being nimble and able to respond rapidly to local trends also fattens her bottom line. After noticing that Minneapolis' Somali-American community was booming, she started purchasing books written in Somali with English translations. When she discovered that local schools were ramping up French classes, she stocked more French-English titles.

After Starbucks proved that plenty of customers will pay $4 for a soy-caramel machiatto, many local shops profited from selling equally fancy fare.

Big Chains Bolster Product Demand

Despite all the stores they displaced, the big boxes have also indirectly helped such shops as Beverly's Pet Center thrive. Outlays of billions of dollars for advertising and marketing have bolstered not only the chain brands but also demand for everything from gourmet coffee to home-improvement projects.

In the pet-shop business, firms like Petco helped spark a boom in part by changing people's conception of smelly, helter-skelter pet stores, according to Marshall Meyers, executive vice president of the Pet Industry Joint Advisory Council. After folks found that they adored their new cockatiel, they started going to local shops for accessories unavailable at the chains, he says. The hostility between the independents and the chains has abated somewhat, replaced by a realization that David and Goliath can help each other. Want a hedgehog? You'll have to visit a local pet shop—the big chains haven't a clue how to care for them. For hedgehog food, Petco also accommodates.

The complementary effect may be even more robust in the coffee trade. After Starbucks proved that plenty of customers will pay $4 for a soy-caramel machiatto, many local shops profited from selling equally fancy fare. Michael Thomas, co-owner of the Unicorn Cafe in Evanston, Ill., says that after a Starbucks opened across the street from his place in 1992, the increased customer traffic in the neighborhood helped him post his best year ever; his yearly revenues are up 40% since then. "We always felt guilty about raising prices," he says, "but Starbucks helps us do that from time to time."

Many indies have also exploited the Starbucks backlash. Mike Sheldrake, owner of Polly's Gourmet Coffee in Long Beach, Calif., was losing money before he reformatted with an anti-corporate feel, highlighting his giant antique coffee roaster and telling baristas to remember regular customers' names. He has been profitable ever since. "It's as close to a hometown watering hole as you can get," says client Howard Homan, a retired civil servant.

The indies' success hasn't escaped the chains' notice. Both Home Depot and Borders Books & Music are experimenting with smaller-format stores. Home Depots are supposed to become more user friendly, especially for women, who perform a growing proportion of home-improvement jobs and have been instrumental in Lowe's rapid growth. But the best-run indies should continue to stay ahead of the competition if they're mindful of the old bear joke: Two guys are backpacking and notice a bear approaching. One guy drops his backpack and starts running, while his buddy stays put, frozen in fear. "You can't outrun a bear," shouts the guy standing still. "I know," replies the sprinter. "I just have to outrun you."

7

Wal-Mart Exploits Workers and Communities

Dan Coleman

Dan Coleman spent many years as a political columnist for the Chapel Hill (NC) Herald. He now lives in Iowa City, where he remains active in the Iowa Green Party, a political party focused on environmental and grassroots issues.

Wal-Mart is a mass-merchandise discount chain with over fifty-three hundred stores across the United States. Many people associate Wal-Mart with low prices. These "bargains," however, come at a very high price to the workers and their communities. Many Wal-Mart employees earn so little pay that they must depend on public assistance. As a result, taxpayers end up paying more to the government to pay for welfare benefits. In addition, Wal-Mart treats employees poorly to create high turnover because the longer they work at Wal-Mart, the more the company has to raise their wages and increase benefits such as health insurance. Moreover, Wal-Mart has continually broken labor laws by not allowing workers to form a union. Wal-Mart also outsources U.S. jobs to China and drives local stores out of business. The public must create a movement to end Wal-Mart's unethical business practices.

On July 28, [2005,] I joined nearly 200 residents of Chatham and Orange counties [in North Carolina] who packed themselves into the dining room of Dockside Restaurant near the county line. The last time I witnessed a cross-

Dan Coleman, "What's Wrong with Wal-Mart?" *Independent Weekly*, November 9, 2005. Reproduced by permission of the author.

county gathering of this scale was in 1986 when citizens waged a pitched battle to prevent the licensing of the Shearon Harris Nuclear Power Plant.

This time the threat was Wal-Mart. Those gathered at Dockside were concerned about its impact on the local economy, its association with sprawl, its treatment of workers, and with the global role of the Arkansas-based behemoth.

Although the world's largest retailer lacks the dramatically explosive potential of a nuclear power plant, its impact has been devastating to communities across the United States. It has played a major role in the dismantling of America's manufacturing base and the disappearance of the middle-class worker.

[Wal-Mart] is a corporation that seeks to maintain profits by keeping its employees on the edge of poverty.

Wal-Mart's Suspect Practices

Although the feared North Chatham Supercenter has yet to appear and things have been quiet lately along the Orange-Chatham line, Wal-Mart is again in the news. [In October 2005], the nonprofit group Wal-Mart Watch obtained a memo to the company's board of directors written by its executive vice president for benefits, Susan Chambers.

The memo confirms what anti-Wal-Mart activists have been claiming for years: that pay, benefits and working conditions at Wal-Mart are bad, and intentionally so. This is a corporation that seeks to maintain profits by keeping its employees on the edge of poverty.

And that's not all. As Robert Greenwald's new film *Wal-Mart: The High Cost of Low Price* (www.walmartmovie.com) dramatically illustrates, Wal-Mart is complicit in the evisceration of main streets across the United States. Its policies drive local stores and American manufacturers out of business. The retail giant has been charged with a wide range of abuses, at home and abroad.

Wal-Mart's success is a matter of legend. As [journalist] Simon Head put it in the [December 16, 2004,] *New York Review of Books*, "With 1.4 million employees worldwide, Wal-Mart's workforce is now larger than that of GM, Ford, GE, and IBM combined. At $258 billion in 2003, Wal-Mart's annual revenues are 2 percent of U.S. GDP [gross domestic product] and eight times the size of Microsoft's. In fact, when ranked by its revenues, Wal-Mart is the world's largest corporation."

Because of Wal-Mart's size and economic clout, its low standards drive down those of other companies—or it drives them out of business completely. Even the most self-interested Americans should be concerned about Wal-Mart's employment practices—someday, someone you love may have no option other than a Wal-Mart style job.

Now ..., Americans are waking up and fighting back. The release of the Greenwald film is only the first step in ... a campaign in which Wal-Mart Watch, along with partners like Sierra Club and SEIU [Service Employees International Union], is coordinating a coalition of over 400 organizations to raise awareness about the problems associated with this economic behemoth.

Wal-Mart provides employees with instruction on how to apply for public assistance programs like food stamps and state health insurance for the poor.

Wal-Mart Costs Taxpayers Money

In the midst of what *Business Week* has termed "A Stepped-Up Assault on Wal-Mart," Susan Chambers' memo to her board of directors couldn't come at a worse time for the Arkansas-based corporation.

Chambers tells the directors that "Wal-Mart has a significant percentage of associates and their children on public assistance." According to Liza Featherstone's book *Selling Women Short*, packed in the envelope with their meager paychecks, Wal-Mart provides employees with instruction on how to apply for public assistance programs like food stamps and state health insurance for the poor.

A congressional study discovered that for a 200-employee Wal-Mart store, the government is spending $108,000 a year for children's health care; $125,000 a year in tax credits and deductions for low-income families; and $42,000 a year in housing assistance. This typical Wal-Mart store costs federal taxpayers $420,000 a year, which averages out to $2,103 for each Wal-Mart employee. It all adds up to an annual welfare bill of $2.5 billion for Wal-Mart's 1.2 million U.S. employees. That's not counting the burden Wal-Mart places on state and local governments.

Wal-Mart has long depended on high turn-over, with some 50 percent of its employees departing before they were eligible for benefits. Even so, the memo from Wal-Mart's Susan Chambers expressed concern that workers were staying too long, thereby pushing up wage and benefit costs, although she stopped short of calling for efforts to push out more senior workers.

She wrote that "the cost of an associate with seven years of tenure is almost 55 percent more than the cost of an associate with one year of tenure, yet there is no difference in his or her productivity. Moreover, because we pay an associate more in salary and benefits as his or her tenure increases, we are pricing that associate out of the labor market, increasing the likelihood that he or she will stay with Wal-Mart."

So much for the quaint idea that workers who do a good job at successful businesses should have some measure of job security.

Health Care for Workers Is Inadequate

The New York Times reported on the memo a mere four days after its business section ran a story on Wal-Mart's plan to expand its health care offerings. Turns out they need it. The Chambers memo states that workers "are getting sicker than the national population, particularly in obesity-related diseases." Like the uninsured in general, Wal-Mart workers tend to overuse emergency rooms and under-use prescriptions and doctor visits.

According to [consumer advocate] Ralph Nader, although Wal-Mart requires an employee to work 34 hours a week to qualify as full time, the average workweek is only 32 hours. Part-time workers have to wait two years to qualify for insurance. Given the high turnover, few workers even reach eligibility. Of those who qualify, not many are willing to pay a premium that, under the current system, takes one-fifth of the average paycheck.

While the new proposal would cost workers only $11 per month, it would have limited coverage the first year and a very high deductible. Critics have called it a plan that only makes sense for healthy people.

Workers Have Poor Morale

We have yet to see an internal memo documenting Wal-Mart's practice of discrimination against women. According to Liza Featherstone, sexism is widespread at Wal-Mart. She reviews patterns of denial of promotion opportunities to women, underpayment of female employees, and the prevalence of exclusive, men-only meetings. Barbara Ehrenreich reports similar abuses in her book *Nickel and Dimed*.

Wal-Mart's working conditions take their toll on employees. According to Simon Head's article in the *New York Review of Books*, "[I]t is hard for Wal-Mart employees to take pride in their work or to have confidence in themselves ... With its deliberate understaffing, its obsession about time theft, its anagement spies, and its arbitrary punishments, Wal-Mart is a workplace where management's suspicion can affect the morale of even the best employees, creating a discrepancy between their objective record of high productivity and how they come to regard their performance on the job as a result of their day-to-day dealings with management. This discrepancy helps keep wages and benefits low at Wal-Mart."

Wal-Mart flouts state and federal laws that protect labor organizing. According to *Mother Jones* [magazine], the National Labor Relations Board has ruled that Wal-Mart repeatedly broke the law by interrogating workers, confiscating union literature and firing union supporters. At the first sign of organizing in a store, Wal-Mart dispatches a team of union busters from its headquarters in Bentonville, Ark., sometimes setting up surveillance cameras to monitor workers.

"In my 35 years in labor relations, I've never seen a company that will go to the lengths that Wal-Mart goes to, to avoid a union," said Martin Levitt, a management consultant who helped the company develop its anti-union tactics before writing a book called *Confessions of a Union Buster.* "They have zero tolerance."

Wal-Mart Takes Away U.S. Jobs

Wal-Mart works relentlessly to find low-cost production facilities overseas. In doing so it has no regard for the consequences for American businesses or workers despite being called by *Fortune* [magazine] "America's most admired corporation."

Hedrick Smith's *Frontline* documentary "Is Wal-Mart Good for America?" tells of Circleville, Ohio, where the local RCA plant was once a source of good jobs with good pay and benefits. In 2003, RCA's owner, Thomson Consumer Electronics, lost a sizeable portion of its production orders and six months later shut the plant down, throwing 1,000 people out of work. The reason: Wal-Mart was now purchasing those products from China.

With tragic irony, a Wal-Mart Supercenter is now going up next to the empty Thomson plant. It will offer poverty wages to middle-aged workers who once earned good salaries in the manufacturing sector. Asked what the future held for kids coming out of high school, Circleville's mayor shook his head and said, "We don't know. We don't know."

When U.S. producers attempt to use our laws to protect themselves, Wal-Mart can be counted on to lend a hand—to the Chinese. Five Rivers Electronics is an American TV manufacturer that sued the Chinese for unfair trade practices. Wal-Mart filed a brief opposing Five Rivers' action. "Why would Wal-Mart testify to support jobs in China instead of American jobs?" asks Five Rivers President Thomas Hopson.

"Wal-Mart and China are a joint venture" is the answer given to *Frontline* by Duke professor Gary Gereffi, an expert in retail chains. China uses Wal-Mart to break open the U.S. market; Wal-Mart turns to Chinese factories for goods to sell at "unbeatable" low prices. . . .

Wal-Mart tricks consumers by offering a small number of high-profile products at rock-bottom prices.

Wal-Mart vs. Local Business

But what about closer to home? Wal-Mart has a long history of using predatory pricing to drive local competition out of business. According to *Forbes* [magazine], for every new Wal-Mart, two rival supermarkets will close.

Often Wal-Mart will open a store close to town until the competition dries up. Then that store is closed and moved to a larger space perhaps closer to an interstate.

Wal-Mart opened a Supercenter in Hillsborough [Florida in 2004]. Their old store remains empty. The reason: Wal-Mart controls the lease through 2009 and can keep out any prospective competition.

Wal-Mart Is No Good for Communities

Still, some communities clamor for Wal-Mart and the jobs it promises. However, a study released [in October 2005] by David Neumark of the Public Policy Institute of California contends that Wal-Mart stores reduce employment by anywhere from 2 to 4 percent and depress local wages by as much as 5 percent.

Those who defend Wal-Mart say it meets the needs of the poor for low-cost goods. In fact, Wal-Mart tricks consumers by offering a small number of high-profile products at rock-bottom prices. These are loss-leaders to lure shoppers into departments where they often select less competitively priced alternatives. And, as the competition leaves town, Wal-Mart's low prices are right behind.

Still, there is a cottage industry in justifying obscene profits, the loss of livable income jobs, and unethical production practices using the "helps the poor" rationale. Such calculations usually leave out a number of factors, including:

- The full, systemic environmental cost of shipping products from China and other distant lands.

- The full environmental cost of our travel to make big-box purchases.

- The life-cycle costs of short-lived products that low-income consumers purchase because they appear to be less expensive.

- The health costs associated with the typically highly processed foods that are available at big box stores.

- The cost to communities where stable local businesses are driven under by big-box competition.

- The waste processing and disposal cost of the packaging and non-reusable, non-repairable, non-recyclable goods sold at big box stores.

- The costs, detailed above, to taxpayers for public assistance for Wal-Mart employees.

Thus, big-box retail Wal-Mart style is a shell game in which costs are shifted to the public while profits accumulate in the Walton family coffers. The challenge to those who seek a socially responsible and environmentally sustainable economy is to develop systems that assign these costs to the corporations that create them, thus transforming Wal-Mart's "really low prices" into really accurate prices.

In the meantime, a movement is needed for socially responsible production, retail and consumption. To a great extent that will depend on businesses identifying themselves as such and organizing mutual support and public outreach networks. But just as important will be a citizens' movement that goes beyond the formidable task of stopping Wal-Mart to demanding and supporting the creation of an ethically sound economy.

8

Wal-Mart Supports Communities

Don Longo

Don Longo is the director of editorial and content development for the Retail Group of VNU Business Publications.

The media is ignoring the contribution that Wal-Mart makes to communities. Wal-Mart offers communities employment with competitive wages, as well as maintaining aggressive pricing models.

While much of the consumer and business press wrings its hands over Wal-Mart's remarkable success, few media outlets are pointing out the positive contributions that the world's largest company makes to the retail industry and the entire consumer goods market.

At a meeting last month in Little Rock, AR, Wal-Mart president and CEO Lee Scott acknowledged that the negative press coverage is partly the retailer's own fault for not getting its message out aggressively enough. "We have to get more aggressive," Scott told an audience at the Arkansas Statehouse Convention Center during the Little Rock Regional Chamber of Commerce's Fortune 500 luncheon. The comments came in the aftermath of Wal-Mart's loss of a ballot initiative to build a supercenter in Inglewood, CA.

While Wal-Mart views much of the coverage it gets as unfair, the long-term effect of the negative press coverage on the

Don Longo, "Fighting a Bad Rap: Wal-Mart's Positive Contributions to Retailing and Local Communities Are Often Overlooked by Sensation-seeking Press and Special Interests," *Retail Merchandiser*, 2004. Reproduced by permission.

retailer's fortunes is debatable. Despite growing community opposition, Wal-Mart still plans to add 330 to 350 stores this year, including Sam's Clubs and Neighborhood Markets, for a total of about 50 million sq. ft. of retail space in the U.S.

But, some industry watchers say the unrelenting bashing in the press will eventually undermine consumers' trust in a company that at one time was almost universally portrayed as a quintessential American success story. Others minimize the effect, saying consumers realize that Wal-Mart's sheer size makes it a convenient target of labor unions and other special interests.

Speaking at a recent magazine publishers' conference, Wal-Mart's SVP for general merchandise, Gordon Erickson, insisted that the retailer's customers "understand we're not an amazingly monstrous company taking over the world . . . What you read and what we are are two different things."

Forty percent of industry professionals that answered a monthly poll on the Retail Merchandiser Web site (www.retailmerchandiser.com) last month, felt continued bashing in the consumer press will have "some negative effect" on the future of Wal-Mart, but they also were confident that "Wal-Mart will be able to counter [this effect] by better publicizing its good deeds and the positive contributions it makes to communities." That Wal-Mart must get its message out to consumers and the media more effectively is plainly evident. The ballot measure in Inglewood, a Los Angeles suburb whose population is more than 93% Black and Hispanic, is a good example. Voters defeated the measure by a two-to-one margin, despite the promise of 1,200 jobs and millions of dollars in sales tax revenue. As has been the case in recent years, opposition to the supercenter was led by labor unions that view the non-union mass retailer as a threat. What was unusual about this defeat, though, was the participation of religious groups and outsiders, like the Rev. Jesse Jackson, who threatened legal action against Wal-Mart if voters approved the measure.

In an exclusive interview, Michael Duke, president and CEO of the Wal-Mart Stores division of Wal-Mart, agreed to talk to Retail Merchandiser about Wal-Mart's impact on the American economy and life.

Impact on Wages

RM: As America's largest private employer, Wal-Mart is often blamed for shifting workers from higher paying jobs to lower paying retail jobs. Is Wal-Mart's growth holding down the annual earnings of American workers?

A little known fact that has always been true of Wal-Mart . . . is that two-thirds of our managers started as hourly associates.

Michael Duke: "People who write about the quality of jobs at Wal-Mart don't understand or know anything about our associates. I am amazed at the inaccuracies I see. When you get to know our people, their dedication and loyalty, and you see first-hand their level of commitment, you realize these are quality jobs.

"It's interesting to see the great demand there is for Wal-Mart positions. We opened a store last year in Valley Stream [a Long Island suburb just across the New York City border] where we had over 15,000 applicants for 300 jobs. They all wanted to wear that Wal-Mart badge. When I visit with our associates, I can see their pride. They know they were the very best from more than 15,000 applicants. They feel like the chosen ones.

"A little known fact that has always been true of Wal-Mart, and is still true today, is that two-thirds of our managers started as hourly associates. So our people see the long-range opportunity of working at Wal-Mart. This year, we will promote more than 9,000 hourly associates into managerial positions in the U.S.

"Our employee turnover rate is decreasing year-to-year [*Business Week* recently reported that hourly employee turnover rate was 44% annually last year at Wal-Mart] and we still feel that our people make the difference."

Duke is passionate when he talks about Wal-Mart associates. "Just yesterday, a 27-year-old associate was enthusiastically talking about owning stock in the company with another associate who has only been with us a few months. The majority of our associates participate in our discount stock purchase program," said Duke. Critics of Wal-Mart's low hourly wages seldom mention the armies of executive positions—including VPS, SVPS and divisional leader—created by the retailer's growth.

Critics seldom talk about how households in communities all over the U.S. are struggling to make ends meet and how Wal-Mart provides a solution for tight budgets.

Impact on Communities

RM: The Inglewood controversy is only the latest in a number of challenges by local community groups to Wal-Mart expansion. The "Stop Wal-Mart" movement claims that any increase in employment, sales and property-tax receipts is offset by job losses at competitors and other business closings. In what ways does Wal-Mart have a positive effect on the communities in which it operates?

Duke: "You only read about the problems. You don't read about all the elected officials who write and ask us to open a store in their municipality. There are a number of facts to look at. In California, we really are helping to improve the standard of living wherever we can serve customers in that state. A recent study conducted by an outside research firm for the Los Angeles Economic Development Council found that if Wal-Mart could achieve a 20% market share, consumers in the City of Los Angeles would achieve a savings of $668 million."

Critics seldom talk about how households in communities all over the U.S. are struggling to make ends meet and how Wal-Mart provides a solution for tight budgets.

"With the taxes that we pay on the local, state and federal levels, we are welcomed in many more cases than not," said Duke. "Warren Buffett was quoted in *Fortune* magazine last year saying, 'You can add it all up and they [Wal-Mart] have contributed $10 billion in annual savings to the financial well-being of Americans.' And, Michael Cox, chief economist for the Federal Reserve Bank of Dallas was quoted in the *New York Times* saying, 'Wal-Mart is the greatest thing that happened to low income Americans.'"

Duke also acknowledges the need for Wal-Mart to do a better job communicating its message. Referring to recent television ads that spotlight Wal-Mart's store in Baldwin Hills, CA—a depressed area of Los Angeles—Duke said: "I think we are making an attempt to let people know who we really are. We want people to know the truth."

Impact on Suppliers

RM: Wal-Mart's relentless pricing pressure forces suppliers to change product specifications, conform to Wal-Mart-dictated delivery schedules and manage inventory to a degree not demanded by other retailers. On the other hand, Wal-Mart does not charge slotting fees and shares more data with suppliers than other retailers do. Now, with Wal-Mart leading the charge into RFID [Radio Frequency Identification], what do suppliers need to understand in order to maximize their relationship with the retailer?

Duke: "I meet with suppliers every week. We have a great relationship and we get great support from our suppliers. When I speak with them, I put a lot of emphasis on Wal-

Mart's open door policy. It's not just for associates. We want suppliers to come to us so we can hear and discuss problems. This year, Wal-Mart was again ranked No. I among retailers in Cannondale Associates' annual anonymous poll of suppliers. Suppliers like it that we deal straight up and honestly with them. Our policies against gifts and gratuities set the highest standards in the retail industry.

"Our RFID initiative has been a team effort with suppliers from the start. As with all things, we've asked them to talk with us about any concerns and strive to find ROI [return of investment] within their own organizations. We've already held meetings with 110-plus suppliers about RFID and are optimistic about our discussions. We've assigned a Wal-Mart executive sponsor and a Wal-Mart program sponsor to all suppliers so we can work together to make this initiative successful."

We are not the driving force for creating off-shore jobs. The consumer chooses quality and value—that is what drives retailing today.

Sending Jobs Overseas

RM: Critics also argue that Wal-Mart's global pursuit of low-cost goods is partly to blame for accelerating the loss of U.S. manufacturing jobs to China and other low-wage nations. How is this a good thing for America?

Duke: "We are not the driving force for creating off-shore jobs. The consumer chooses quality and value—that is what drives retailing today.

"In the countries where we operate stores, we offer customers every day low prices for the food and other things that they need in their daily lives. In many cases, these prices are significantly lower than those offered by other retailers. In other cases, our low prices cause other retailers to lower their own prices. In both cases, the customer benefits. The customer's standard of living is raised because he/she can purchase more for the same amount of money. This is very, very important to people struggling to make ends meet from paycheck to paycheck. In addition, Wal-Mart pay and benefits are always competitive in the markets where we operate. If we did otherwise, we could not attract the good associates we rely upon to deliver superior service to our customers.

"In the countries where our suppliers produce goods, we raise the standard of living by offering jobs that are often significantly better than others available to workers in the area. We are strict in requiring our suppliers to follow wage and hourly standards and we take corrective actions if we discover improper payment of regular wages or overtime. We take other positive steps, such as adding child-care facilities at the majority of factories we utilize in Bangladesh and insisting that workers in China receive paid annual and maternity leave according to local laws."

Left unsaid is the impact that global sourcing has had on helping to create a working class and more hopeful future for workers in many poverty-stricken countries around the world.

It is unusual for Wal-Mart to be so concerned about how it is portrayed in the media. Rising fuel prices, the rising cost of health care for workers, the lack of meaningful class-action lawsuit reform, and how its established retail model will be accepted as it expands into a growing list of foreign countries are other issues that keep Wal-Mart executives up at night. But, for the immediate future, look for Wal-Mart to turn up the volume on its marketing and public relations efforts to promote its positive effect on workers, suppliers and customers.

9

Many Consumers Prefer Chain Stores

Russell Roberts

Russell Roberts is a professor of economics at George Mason University. He also has taught at the University of Rochester, Stanford University, and UCLA. Roberts can often be heard on National Public Radio's Morning Edition *program and writes for both the* New York Times *and the* Wall Street Journal.

Most Americans are quick to lament the closing of mom-and-pop shops. They are a symbol of old-town charm and a different way of life. It is easy to blame chain stores for the demise of these shops, but consumers are really the ones responsible for closing down local stores by their willingness to shop at chain stores. The convenience, selection, and value of a Barnes & Noble or a Home Depot often outweigh the charm of a local bookstore or hardware store in the eyes of shoppers. Chain stores also allow people to save a lot of money that can be used for sending their children to college or donated to charity.

Near where I live is a charming little stretch of shops called "the Loop" that caters to students and the university community. There are bars and restaurants and a gorgeous restored movie theater from the 1920s and a bike shop and a juice bar and a used book store and a vintage clothing store and a used CD store and you get the idea. In many ways, it's much nicer than it was when I moved here a dozen years ago. The stores are a little more upscale and everything is cleaner and nicer as older buildings have been renovated.

Russell Roberts, "Do 'Big Box' Retailers Harm the Quality of Life?" *Library of Economics and Liberty*, June 25, 2001. Reproduced by permission of the author.

The Loop is about a ten-minute walk from my house. We love being able to walk there and we're happy it's nicer than it was when we first arrived. But in another dimension, the Loop is not as nice. Two wonderful stores have gone out of business and have not been replaced: a lovely independent bookstore called Paul's Books, and Smith Hardware, one of those phenomenal hardware stores where the owner and his daughter knew everything from bird seed to PVC pipe. Paradoxically, the best way to describe Smith Hardware is the smell. You can't convey smell in print or online, but it doesn't matter. You know what a hardware store like Smith Hardware smells like. It's that mix of mulch, bug spray, and who knows what else.

My kids will never know that smell. To them, a hardware store looks and smells like Home Depot. Home Depot may have a few spots that smell like Smith's, but it's too big and diverse a place to have a single smell. Home Depot destroyed Smith Hardware, and a Barnes & Noble superstore about three miles away destroyed Paul's Books. Home Depot and Barnes & Noble are typical "big box" retailers, enormous stores with enormous inventories that strike fear into the heart of small, independent merchants. So now if I want a book or just want to browse, or if I want to replace the mechanism inside my toilet or pick up some wood screws to repair a piece of furniture, I have to get in my car.

No one forced us to shop at Home Depot and Barnes and Noble. And nobody stopped us either. We made the choices.

Lured by Chain Stores

So who is to blame for the demise of Paul's Books and Smith Hardware? I said a moment ago that they were destroyed by Barnes & Noble and Home Depot, but that's hyperbole designed to lull the reader into a false sense of economics. I was just testing you. If I really want to find the culprit, he's easy enough to spot. I see him in the mirror every morning. I put Paul's and Smith out of business. Oh sure. I shopped there from time to time. But when I wanted a book that Paul's didn't have, I would get it at Barnes & Noble rather than have Paul's order it. And while I was there, I might pick up a few others as well, ones I could have bought at Paul's on another visit.

And if I wanted to fix the toilet at ten o'clock at night, sometimes I'd just get in my car and go to Home Depot. They're open 24 hours a day. And they have everything. In profusion. In every size. I love walking around there and I'm not even a fixit type. My children will never know what Smith Hardware smells like, but they know what Home Depot sounds like. I used to take my oldest son there as a toddler. We'd hear the whine of the forklift and race our cart over to the appropriate aisle and watch it pull down a pallet from the ceiling.

And while I was picking up the piece to fix the toilet, I'd stock up on light bulbs at a fraction of the price that Smith charged. And they'd have every kind I needed, even the weird halogen ones for the living room.

There must be a lot of people like me—people who liked Paul's and Smith but who found themselves shopping there less often than they once did. No one forced us to shop at Home Depot and Barnes & Noble. And nobody stopped us either. We made the choices we thought were best for us at the time.

Some People Do Not Miss the Small Stores

You could argue that if we had realized that our choices had consequences beyond the price of those halogen bulbs, we might have shopped more at Paul's and Smith. That is, you could argue that if I and all the other shoppers had known that we were destroying Paul's and Smith, we might have made a different decision. We didn't realize that each of our small wounds to the bottom line of Paul's and Smith summed up to mortal blows. If we had realized that, we would have been more loyal, Paul's and Smith would still be around, the Loop would be a nicer place and we'd be happier.

You can make that argument, but it's hard to marshal any evidence for it other than a wispy desire on my part to be able to walk to my hardware store. I do miss Paul's and Smith, but frankly, not that much. Not enough to give up the benefits of Home Depot and Barnes & Noble. And I suspect the non-romantics among my neighbors miss them not at all. A lot of people actually enjoy driving to stores rather than walking. They don't like to walk back with a backpack or shopping bag, lugging those purchases. And I respect that set of preferences along with my own.

But there are folks on the other side of me on the romance-of-small-business spectrum as well. Folks who would never shop at Barnes & Noble or Home Depot even to save money or time because they were loyal to Paul's and Smith. Their lives are diminished a little by their departure. And it is those people who make the most noise when small businesses go under. When the local coffee shop that is full of charm gets replaced by a Starbucks, some of those folks are genuinely sad.

Because of Home Depot and Wal-Mart and all these other corporate behemoths, people have saved a lot of money.

Chain Stores Have Benefited America

I'd like to cheer up the people who decry the homogenization of America. I'd like to cheer up the people who despise the big boxes on the edge of town and the corporate machines—the Home Depots and Wal-Marts and Costcos and Starbucks—who crowd out the little guys.

Here are my words of consolation:

You worry that the world is getting less interesting. You worry that when Main Street gets replaced by Edge City that something intangible is lost. You may be right. But there are some intangibles (and tangibles) on the plus side as well.

Think of all the people in the small towns of America who before Wal-Mart came along had to shop in dingy general stores on Main Street with high prices and poor selection. When Wal-Mart came to town, the people in those towns whooped and cheered. Because of Starbucks, some people have access to the first intensely flavorful cup of coffee they've ever had outside their home, maybe even their first great cup of coffee ever. Because of Barnes & Noble, people can shop among 100,000 books.

And because of Home Depot and Wal-Mart and all these other corporate behemoths, people have saved a lot of money. It's only money, but having more money left over after shopping creates all kinds of other activities and businesses that are hidden but real. They've used all that money they once spent on higher-priced hardware and underwear and used it to do all kinds of glorious things we can't see but can only imagine, sending kids to college or giving them music lessons, buying a nicer house or taking a longer vacation, funding a charity or contributing to a political cause. The left-over spending power has flowed into a million other places, allowing all kinds of businesses and non-profits to get a start they wouldn't have had if retailing hadn't gotten more efficient and cheaper.

New Opportunities

Finally, think of Mr. Smith's daughter. Like Mr. Smith, she knew everything about everything you needed to know. She may be miserable now or thrilled that the store is gone. Its closing may have liberated her or punished her. We don't know. But think about her children, if she has any. They may have dreamed of working in a hardware store like their mother and grandfather. But there is a chance, and my guess is that it's more than an even chance, that they would dream of doing something else.

Because of the efficiency of Wal-Mart and Home Depot and Barnes & Noble, fewer resources and management talent are involved in retailing and more are available elsewhere. That means more opportunity for the next generation. That is the true fruit of economic change, and most of us, maybe almost all of us, want our children and our children's children to be able to enjoy it.

So for most of us, even many of us who miss Paul's Books and Smith Hardware, there are many consolations. The world of economic change is full of hidden delights that sweeten the sorrow of saying goodbye to Paul's Books and Smith Hardware.

10

Many Consumers Reject Chain Stores

Jay Walljasper

Jay Walljasper is director of strategic communications for the organization Project for Public Spaces (PPS). PPS studies public places such as parks, plazas, and central squares in order to turn them into viable community areas. Walljasper has written several articles and essays on urban planning and also writes a weekly column for the PPS newsletter Making Places.

When a retail behemoth like Wal-Mart comes to town, some local stores simply close down their businesses to avoid a long, drawn-out battle with the retailer. For a long time, this destruction of local stores seemed inevitable. However, now it appears attitudes are changing. More and more people are choosing to shop at locally owned businesses rather than at homogeneous chain stores. Across the country, independent coffee shops, diners, and retail stores are thriving. By supporting local businesses, both the consumer and the community benefit.

Even with all that PPS [Project for Public Spaces] and its partners have accomplished over three decades in showing how the power of place can transform our communities, the idea of Placemaking [creating sustainable public places that build communities] still faces formidable obstacles. The old thinking that bigger is better remains strong across the country.

The Placemaking movement that PPS and friends are now launching has its hands full questioning mega-development

Jay Walljasper, *Making Places Newsletter*, February 2006. Reproduced by permission of the author (www.pps.org).

proposals, challenging road expansion plans, and debunking "design-for-design's sake" architecture. But the most dramatic sign of what we are up against is the proliferation of big box retail, which knocks the life out of downtowns everywhere and sucks the economic and cultural vitality out of many communities. The most potent symbol of what's threatening American places and communities today is, without a doubt, Wal-Mart.

Wal-Mart Shuts Down Local Businesses

Many locally-owned stores simply shut their doors at the first sign of Wal-Mart, rather than prolong the misery of trying to compete against this giant. You can see the results in boarded-up Main Streets and neighborhood shopping districts across the continent. In Iowa alone, according to noted environmental writer Bill McKibben, Wal-Mart wiped out 555 groceries, 298 hardware stores, 293 building supply stores, 161 variety stores, 158 women's clothing stores, 153 shoe stores, 116 drug stores, and 111 men's and boys' clothing stores in a ten-year period. Life in these places has changed drastically, now that local shoppers' money flows out of town rather than circulating around the community again and again through locally-owned businesses.

Americans are growing weary of the coast-to-coast sameness of big chains and want to patronize places that express the personality of their communities.

Many believe this is the inevitable march of history, with independent businesses being trampled into extinction everywhere. But that's not what happened in Powell, Wyoming. Despite a Wal-Mart in a nearby town, a clothing store called Powell Mercantile has thrived. That's because it is owned by the community itself. Five hundred citizens put up money to launch the store because they didn't want to see their Main

Street boarded up. Indeed the store's success has started a chain reaction, with other shops opening up in once empty downtown locations. Powell has come back to life. And now the town of Worland, ninety miles south, is doing the same thing.

Local Businesses Are Making a Comeback

Rather than a relic of the Norman Rockwell past, I think Powell Mercantile is a beacon of positive trends to come. Americans are growing weary of the coast-to-coast sameness of big chains and want to patronize places that express the personality of their communities. You hear a lot about Starbucks and Hard Rock Cafés these days, but as I travel the country I find all kinds of independent coffee shops and bars, with gloriously mismatched furniture, homemade food and local beers. They often sit next door to one-of-a-kind businesses like vintage clothing stores, used bookshops, art galleries, health food groceries, music clubs, antique dealers, gift shops, ethnic eateries, and burger joints. Indeed, some of them are banding together in organizations like the new American Independent Business Alliance (http://www.amiba.net/) to make a powerful case why locally-owned businesses are essential to the future of America's economy and culture.

I see this happening in my own neighborhood, the Kingfield district of south Minneapolis, where 1910s-era bungalows and Craftsmen-style homes have attracted many young families. We've enjoyed a revival of small businesses over the past 10 years as new shops and restaurants pop up in old storefronts, most of them run by people living in the neighborhood.

A few blocks from my house I've got Roadrunner Records, where you'll find few CDs by the likes of Britney Spears, Alan Jackson or Eminem. But almost every other musical genre imaginable is in abundance—from Renaissance dances to Cajun classics to obscure gems of grunge rock. Across the street is Anodyne, a bustling coffee shop that I have never once entered without spotting a friend, neighbor or old acquaintance. Down the street is Odds N Ends, an antique store with an impeccable collection of topnotch bric-a-brac, curious paintings, and a broad selection of great old rugs—at prices you can actually afford.

Strolling a different direction from my house brings you to Bakery on Grand, with baguettes and semolina loaves so good I'm convinced low-carb diets are a crime against humanity. Then there's Victor's 1959 Café, a cool Cuban diner where a sign encourages you to sit in booths on either the left wing (Che posters) or the right wing (Free Elian posters). Catty-corner from there is the Fairy Godmother store, a marvelous selection of books, gifts and other fun items that remind us the world is still full of magic and mystery. And speaking of mystery, down the block stands an inscrutable junk shop with no formally agreed upon name, a live-in owner who is open only when the mood strikes him, and precariously steep piles of pop culture treasures everywhere—running the gamut from '50s magazines to old lunch boxes. He also sells solar power supplies over the web. Go figure.

I've found that patronizing independent businesses enriches my life in ways large and small.

Shop Local

Places like these are the social and commercial backbone of our communities. They also expose the lie that independent stores are a thing of the past, destined to go the way of the horse and buggy. Neighborhoods all over North America are now flourishing with vital and valuable locally-owned businesses. The entrepreneurial urge in Americans is strong and can only be extinguished if folks like you and I turn our backs on small, distinctive stores in favor of big, boring boxes.

I've found that patronizing independent businesses enriches my life in ways large and small. Right around the corner from my home is Caffe Tempo, a congenial coffee shop where last week my wife Julie and I ordered eleven dollars and six cents worth of breakfast, tea, and greeting cards before realizing neither of us had brought a wallet. "Don't worry," said the clerk, "just bring it the next time." Imagine that happening at a Starbucks, Denny's, or any other chain more beholden to distant stockholders than its neighbors and customers.

So if you don't want to see your town totally overrun by Wal-Marts, Burger King, and the like, then stand up and make a stand for your local merchants by visiting their stores and buying something. This is one of the basic principles of Placemaking. . . . There's no better time to do it. The future of your community and our country depends on it.

Organizations to Contact

American Economic Foundation (AEF)
50 Public Sq., Suite 1300, Cleveland, OH   44113
(216) 321-6547

AEF is a nonprofit research and educational organization that advocates free-market economic principles. It encourages comprehension and appreciation of the private enterprise system through individual economic self-education. It publishes the economic primer *How We Live*, the leaflet "Ten Pillars of Economic Wisdom," and various booklets and pamphlets.

Business Alliance for Local Living Economies (BALLE)
165 Eleventh St., San Francisco, CA   94103
(415) 255-1108
Web site: www.livingeconomies.org

BALLE is an alliance of independently operated local business networks that work together to develop community-based businesses. It opposes globalization and instead promotes a local living economy. Its publications include the *BALLE Monthly Newsletter*.

Center on National Labor Policy
5211 Port Royal Rd., Suite 103, North Springfield, VA   22151
(703) 321-9180

This public policy group promotes principles of free enterprise in labor policy making. It opposes what it views as the excessive power of unions, seeks to stop government grants to unions and government interference in and regulation of labor policy, and strives to prevent public employee strikes. It publishes the quarterly *Insider's Report*.

Competitive Enterprise Institute (CEI)
1001 Connecticut Ave. NW, Suite 1250
Washington, DC   20036
(202) 331-1010 • fax: (202) 331-0640
e-mail: info@cei.org
Web site: www.cei.org

CEI is a nonprofit organization committed to the principles of free enterprise and limited government. The institute is dedicated to demonstrating that free-market processes and other private initiatives are superior to government intervention in advancing the interests of both producers and consumers. Its publications include *Issue Analysis*.

Corporate Watch
1611 Telegraph Ave., #702, Oakland, CA   94612
(510) 271-8080
e-mail: corpwatch@igc.org
Web site: www.corpwatch.org

Corporate Watch serves as an online magazine and resource center for investigating and analyzing corporate activity. Past articles have included "Blood, Sweat and Shears: Can We Put an End to Sweatshops?" as well as news and action alerts. Its editors are committed to documenting the social, political, economic, and environmental misdeeds committed by corporations and building support for human rights, environmental justice, and democratic control over corporations. Corporate Watch is a project of the Transnational Resource and Action Center, which works to educate people about the social and environmental impact of corporate globalization.

Council on Economic Priorities (CEP)
30 Irving Pl., New York, NY   10003
(212) 420-1133

CEP is a nonprofit public-interest research organization that evaluates and reports on the policies and practices of U.S. and foreign corporations in the areas of the environment, female and minority advancement, disclosure, charitable giving, community outreach, family benefits, and workplace issues. It publishes the books *Shopping for a Better World* and *Students Shopping for a Better World*, the monthly newsletter *Research Report*, and corporate environmental data reports.

Economic Policy Institute (EPI)
1333 H St. NW, Suite 300, East Tower
Washington, DC   20005
e-mail: blustig@epinet.org
Web site: www.epinet.org

EPI conducts research and promotes educational programs on economic policy issues, particularly the economics of poverty, unemployment, and American industry. It supports organized labor and believes that government should invest in infrastructure and education to improve America's economy. It publishes studies and periodic briefing papers as well as the *Economic Policy Institute Journal* three times a year.

Foundation for Economic Education (FEE)
30 S. Broadway, Irvington-on-Hudson, NY   10533
(914) 591-7230
e-mail: comments@fee.org
Web site: www.fee.org

FEE supports the principles of private property, the free market, and limited government. It frequently publishes articles on trade, capitalism, and corporate social responsibility in its monthly magazine, the *Freeman*.

Free Market Project (FMP)
325 S. Patrick St., Alexandria, VA   22314
(703) 683-9733 • fax: (703) 683-9736
e-mail: dgainor@mediaresearch.org
Web site: www.freemarketproject.org

The mission of FMP is to audit the media's coverage of the free enterprise system. It is the project's goal to bring balance to economic reporting and to promote fair portrayal of the business community in the media. Its publications include the weekly newsletter the *Balance Sheet*.

The Heritage Foundation

214 Massachusetts Ave. NE, Washington, DC   20002-4999
(202) 546-4400 • fax: (202) 546-8328
e-mail: info@heritage.org
Web site: www.heritage.org

The foundation is a public policy research institute dedicated to the principles of free competitive enterprise, limited government, individual liberty, and a strong national defense. The foundation publishes the monthly newsletter *Insider; Heritage Today*, a newsletter published six times per year; and various reports and journals.

The New Rules Project

1313 Fifth St. SE, Minneapolis, MN   55414
(612) 379-3815 • fax: (612) 379-3920
e-mail: bailey@ilsr.org
Web site: www.newrules.org

The project strives to create new governmental rules that give people more power within their neighborhoods. It promotes local businesses and the idea of sustainable community. Its publications include the e-newsletter the *Hometown Advantage*.

ReclaimDemocracy.org

222 S. Black Ave., Bozeman, MT   59715
(406) 582-1224
e-mail: info@reclaimdemocracy.org
Web site: www.reclaimdemocracy.org

ReclaimDemocracy.org is dedicated to restoring democratic authority over corporations, reviving grassroots democracy, and revoking the power of money and corporations to control government and civic society. ReclaimDemocracy.org works to support the proliferation and success of small, independent businesses, cooperatives, and employee-owned firms. Its publications include the quarterly newsletter the *Insurgent*.

Sprawl-Busters
21 Grinnell St., Greenfield, MA   01301
(413) 772-6289
e-mail: info@sprawl-busters.com
Web site: www.sprawl-busters.com

Sprawl-Busters helps local communities campaign against me-
gastores and large developments. It argues against overabun-
dance of retail in America and supports local businesses. The
Web site features many articles and reports.

Bibliography

Books

William N. Ander and Neil Z. Stern — *Winning at Retail: Developing a Sustained Model for Retail Success.* Hoboken, NJ: Wiley, 2004.

John U. Bacon — *America's Corner Store: Walgreen's Prescription for Success.* Hoboken, NJ: Wiley, 2004.

Jagdish Bhagwati — *In Defense of Globalization.* New York: Oxford University Press, 2004.

Anthony Bianco — *The Bully of Bentonville.* New York: Doubleday, 2006.

S. Truett Cathy — *Eat Mor Chikin: Inspire More People.* Decatur, GA: Looking Glass, 2002.

John De Graaf, David Wann, and Thomas H. Naylor — *Affluenza: The All-Consuming Epidemic.* San Francisco: Berrett-Koehler, 2005.

Liza Featherstone — *Selling Women Short: The Landmark Battle for Workers Rights at Wal-Mart.* New York: Basic Books, 2004.

Charles Fishman — *The Wal-Mart Effect.* New York: Penguin, 2006.

Jeffrey Hollender and Stephen Fenichell	*What Matters Most: How a Small Group of Pioneers Is Teaching Social Responsibility to Big Business and Why Big Business Is Listening.* New York: Basic Books, 2003.
Greg LeRoy	*The Great American Jobs Scam: Corporate Tax Dodging and the Myth of Job Creation.* San Francisco: Berrett-Koehler, 2005.
George Ritzer	*The McDonaldization of Society.* Thousand Oaks, CA: Sage, 2004.
Laura Rowley	*On Target: How the World's Hottest Retailer Hit a Bull's-Eye.* Hoboken, NJ: Wiley, 2003.
Ann Satterthwaite	*Going Shopping: Consumer Choices and Community Consequences.* New Haven, CT: Yale University Press, 2001.
Michael H. Shuman	*The Small-Mart Revolution: How Local Businesses Are Beating the Global Competition.* San Francisco: Berrett-Koehler, 2006.
John Simmons	*My Sister's a Barista: How They Made Starbucks a Home Away from Home.* London: Cyan, 2005.
Robert Slater	*The Wal-Mart Triumph.* New York: Portfolio Trade, 2004.
Robert Spector	*Category Killers.* Boston: Harvard Business School Press, 2005.

Greg Spotts   *Wal-Mart: The High Cost of Low Prices.* New York: Disinformation, 2005.

Periodicals

Mark W.
Anderson
"Christmas Shopping No Bargain If We Exploit Others," *Columbia Chronicle*, December 6, 2004. www-.columbiachronicle.com

Ted Balaker
"Ban Wal-Mart, Hurt Families," *Los Angeles Daily News*, January 26, 2004.

Rosa Brooks
"Guilty Pleasures, Big-Box Love," *Los Angeles Times*, December 2, 2005.

Zachary Brown
"The Wal-Mart Epidemic: The Case Against Wal-Mart in Vermont," *Vermont Journal of Environmental Law*, April 13, 2005.

Economist
"Opening Up the Big Box," February 23, 2006.

T.A. Frank
"Everyday Low Vices," *Washington Monthly*, April 2006.

Christine Frey
"Costco's Love of Labor: Employees' Well-Being Key to Its Success," *Seattle Post-Intelligencer*, March 29, 2004.

Stephan J. Goetz
"Big-Boxes and Economic Development," *Network04*, December 2004.

Steven
Greenhouse
"How Costco Became the Anti-Wal-Mart," *New York Times*, July 17, 2005.

Markel Hutchins   "Defense of Wal-Mart a Low Blow—Always," *Atlanta Journal-Constitution*, March 6, 2006.

Paul Krugman   "Big Box Balderdash," *New York Times*, December 12, 2005.

Philip Langdon   "As Retail Chains Grow, Threats to Local Character Increase," *New Urban News*, December 2003. www.newurbannews.com

Devin Leonard   "The Only Lifeline Was the Wal-Mart," *Fortune*, October 3, 2005.

Daniel McGraw   "Giving Away the Store to Get a Store: Tax Increment Financing Is No Bargain for Taxpayers," *Reason*, January 2006.

Stacy Mitchell   "Independent Businesses, Unite!" *In Business*, July/August 2003.

Stacy Mitchell   "When a Giant Retailer Moves On, It Leaves Its 'Big-Box' Behind," *Minneapolis Star Tribune*, January 8, 2001.

Darcy Olsen   "Ice Cream, Anyone?" *Arizona Republic*, July 31, 2005.

Jim Olsztynski   "Competition Is Good for Us," *Roofing Contractor*, January 2004.

Remodeling   "Big Box: Friend or Foe?" October 2005.

Carolyn Said   "Main Street Fights Chain Street," *San Francisco Chronicle*, November 29, 2005.

Amy Stewart   "My Home Town: An Author's Take
                     on the Coming of a Chain," *North
                     Coast Journal*, May 8, 2003. ww-
                     w.northcoastjournal.com

Washington Post   "Don't Ban the Big Box," June 24,
                     2004.

Robert Weissberg   "Wal-Mart: Free to Compete," *LP
                     News*, September 2005. www.lp.org/
                     lpnews

Index